# Animal
## FAVORITES

Please visit our web site at: www.garethstevens.com
For a free color catalog describing Gareth Stevens Publishing's
list of high-quality books and multimedia programs, call
1-800-542-2595 (USA) or 1-800-387-3178 (Canada).
Gareth Stevens Publishing's fax: (414) 332-3567.

Library of Congress Cataloging-in-Publication Data

Bontinck, Helga.
    Animal favorites / Helga Bontinck.—North American ed.
        p. cm. — (Simple steps to drawing)
    Includes bibliographical references.
    ISBN 0-8368-6311-9 (lib. bdg.)
    1. Animals in art—Juvenile literature.  2. Drawing—Technique—Juvenile literature.
    I. Title. II. Series.
    NC780.B59   2006
    743.6—dc22                                          2005040172

This edition first published in 2006 by
**Gareth Stevens Publishing**
A Member of the WRC Media Family of Companies
330 West Olive Street, Suite 100
Milwaukee, Wisconsin  53212  USA

This U.S. edition copyright © 2006 by Gareth Stevens, Inc.  Original edition
copyright © 2005 by Creations for Children International.  First published in 2005
by Creations for Children International, Belgium.

All illustrations by Helga Bontinck

Gareth Stevens editor:  Dorothy L. Gibbs
Gareth Stevens designer:  Scott M. Krall

Printed in the United States of America

1 2 3 4 5 6 7 8 9 10 09 08 07 06

Simple Steps to
**Drawing**

# Animal
## FAVORITES

GARETH**STEVENS**

**GS** PUBLISHING

A Member of the WRC Media Family of Companies

# EASY DRAWING FUN

This book makes drawing easy, even for little hands. Each left-hand page shows you the shapes, lines, and figures you need to make the colorful drawing you see on the right-hand page. Three easy steps show you how to put the shapes together to make a drawing of a butterfly, a hedgehog, a bird singing in a tree, or any of six other animal favorites.

All you have to do is copy the shapes you see in the first box in the order you see them in the boxes labeled 1, 2, 3. After you finish copying the shapes, you will have a simple drawing that you can color or paint to match the picture in the book — or any other way you like.

Get ready. Get set. **DRAW!**

# WHAT YOU WILL NEED

**For drawing, you will need a pencil
and some sheets of plain paper.**
A pencil with soft lead is the best kind for drawing.  An ordinary
No. 2 pencil will work well.  If you use a pencil that is made
specially for drawing, look for one marked HB.  (H means hard lead.
B means soft lead.)  A pencil marked HB is not too hard and not too soft.
Use plain white paper for your drawings.  The colors and paints
you will use to finish your pictures will show up best on white paper.

**For coloring, you will need crayons,
colored pencils, or markers.
For painting, you will need watercolors
or acrylic or poster paints.**
Crayons and colored pencils are easy to use and come in a wide range of
colors.  Markers and paints can be messy so you need to protect your clothing
and your work area.  If you want to paint your drawings,
acrylic and poster paints work best because they dry
quickly.  You can have a lot of fun mixing paint colors.
Even if you start with only red, blue, yellow, and black
paints, you can mix them to make many other colors.
Paintbrushes come in different thicknesses.  You
might want to have two brushes — a thin one and
a thick one.  Be sure to wash your brushes in water
when you are finished painting.

# Butterfly

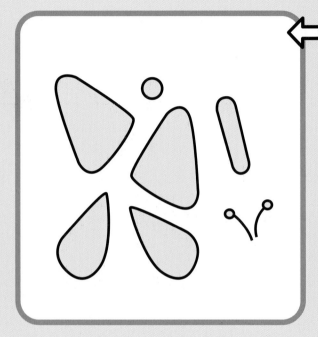

To draw a beautiful butterfly, you will need these shapes and forms.

**1**

**2**

**3**

# Guinea Pig

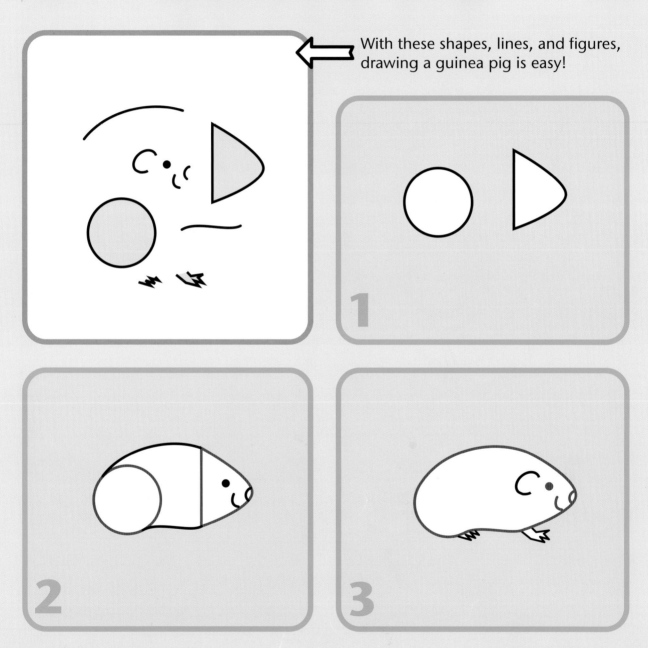

With these shapes, lines, and figures, drawing a guinea pig is easy!

1

2

3

# Sheep

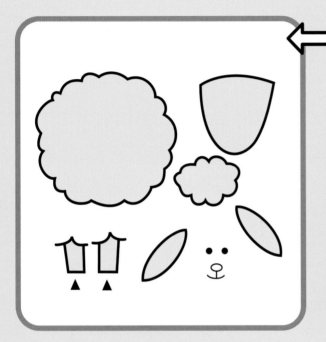

Put these shapes together to draw a fluffy sheep with a curly coat.

**1**

**2**

**3**

# Chicken

With lines, squiggles, and egg-shaped ovals, you can draw a plucky chicken.

1

2

3

13

# Hedgehog

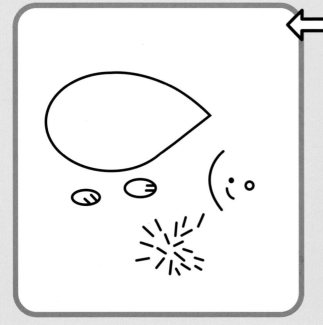

These simple shapes and lines are all you need to draw a smiling hedgehog.

**1**

**2**

**3**

15

# Turtle

Draw a semicircle, then turn it into a turtle with the rest of these easy-to-draw shapes.

**1**

**2**

**3**

# Bird

With these shapes and lines, drawing a bird is as easy as 1, 2, 3.

**1**

**2**

**3**

19

# Honeybee

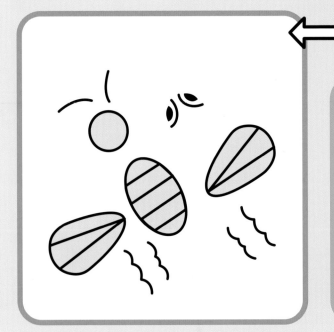

Draw a circle, a few ovals, and some squiggles, spots, and lines to make a busy, buzzy bee.

**1**

**2**

**3**

21

# Kitty Cat

Draw this group of shapes, lines, and figures to make a cuddly kitty.

**1**

**2**

**3**

# MORE EASY DRAWING FUN

## Books

*Dinosaurs.* Easy to Read! Easy to Draw! (series).
   Joan Holub (Price Stern Sloan)

*Drawing with Your Hands.* Drawing Is Easy (series).
   Godeleine De Rosamel (Gareth Stevens)

*I Can Draw Country Animals.* I Can Draw Animals! (series).
   Hélène Leroux-Hugon (Gareth Stevens)

*Let's Draw a House with Shapes.* Let's Draw with Shapes (series).
   Jannel Khu (Rosen's PowerStart Press)

## Web Sites

Draw and Color with Uncle Fred
*www.unclefred.com*

Learn to Draw: A Project 4 Kids
*BillyBear4kids.com/Learn2Draw/Learn2Draw.html*